Sally Warrell was born in Bury St Edmunds where she now lives. She holds a BA in English and Philosophy from Aberystwyth and a BSc in Computer Science from the Open University.

Since childhood she has been writing poetry and prose. In 1987 she published a pamphlet of poetry with two other women, *Songs from Inner Spaces*.
In 2014 she published her first poetry collection, *Cherry Pie and Other Poems*.

She has poems published in *Ink Sweat & Tears*, *@Ease Magazine*, Suffolk Poetry Society and the *Bury Free Press*. She has been a regular contributor to Poetry Aloud since 2008. https://poetryaloud.org.uk. Sally is a member of Suffolk Poetry Society and The Poetry Society.

Sally has worked as an au pair in the South of France, a book keeper, a catering assistant, a washer-upper (Plongeuse) in a hotel in France, a domestic in a London hospital, a housing benefits officer, a civil servant, a part-time lecturer and a hostel worker.
She taught Creative Writing at West Suffolk College for two years. For the past twenty-two years Sally has worked in a library.

Sally Warrell

Collected Poems
1983–2022

ISBN 978-1-909362-62-8

Typeset in Garamond.
Cover artwork © Jasmine Higgins.

Editorial and Design by Kingston University MA Publishing Students: Ashmi Bhatt, Amanda Carungi, Georgina Dent, Jasmine Higgins, Ben Tickner.

KINGSTON UNIVERSITY PRESS
Kingston University
Penrhyn Road
Kingston-upon-Thames
KT1 2EE

For Bill

Contents

Poems featured in the Poetry Aloud third-year
anniversary celebration, 2011

New Poems
2013–2022

From *Songs from Inner Spaces*
Poems 1983–1984

Honey

Where is your soul honey?
In the light of your honey, honey hair?
Where is my bloody heart honey?
It's in your dragon's lair.

Where's the fire in your eyes honey?
Is it in the bowl of your crystal glass?
And why does the whisky burn honey?
Why do you love to flirt?

The Party

(After painting the woodwork of the living room pink)

Deluge
Pink blancmange
Confused lady
Sugar Sadie
Would kill you if she could
Sticky fingers
Sticky lady
She's got the birthday cake blues
Tricky lady
Card sharp lover
The woman torn in six.

The Willow Women

(Inspired by trees in St James Park
and someone I once knew)

Dead white boughs
and leafless twigs,
like the golden and hoary hair
of an ageing woman,
tried, much put upon woman,
weep into the brown khaki of the water
on which a cacophony of black, brown, white, grey,
green birds
skid and swirl.

She can no longer care,
is Gwendoline.

Mandolin memory,
painful nostalgia,
heaps itself on her.

The women at her left side
sway and chant
incantations of her past glory.

Grecian chorus
of women who have not yet lost
their sugar floxed
and sprayed locks.
The candy floss girls
or the washer women
or the brown-haired widow's lament.

On the other side of the water,
on the other side of Lethe,
we still stand tall
and almost unmoving,
Amazons with floating crinolines.

Let us now forget
that we have ever met
or torn or frayed each other.
Let us forget we ever sang.

One who stands alone,
dipping her hands into the lake
to wash away her sins,
puts forth her future life
in a green descant,
arabesque of pale lime shoots,
while gulls in the sunlight
preen on the edge of the water.

Women in a primitive society
bleed inside a cage.

April 1984

I would like to rid myself of this ache of
meaninglessness
this blistering black laburnum pod I call heart,
the endless rattle of the wind in the casements,
whistle along the reaches of the shoreline,
the screaming and flattering of the gulls,
the seeping of sand beneath the door.

Howl! I have lost you. Howl! It is over.

Instead, I light a cigarette and watch
the unchanging scenery of the armchairs
and autumn leaves in the carpet, furling and enfolding
each other
where all my past lives lie buried.

And the play ends as always
with our having to face the un-faceable future,
the void, the mirror of our ever-changing,
and, after all that, unchanged selves.

Ativan Sane

Blue opiate, blue oblivion,
blue horizons,
those shallow seas in which I drown,
not smile, nor frown,
nor feel.

Blue is the colour of sorrow.
Blue is the colour of heartbreak.
Blue is the colour of no more crying.
This slow dying of mind.

Prose Poem

I liked the loneliness of my garret; the restlessness of a welter of ideas, swimming, confused, in the hourglass of night; footsteps, troubled, treading the streets of London (already licked with the tongues of angels, snail trails of white icing – heaven is nailed to hell); the dregs of the coffee, residue of the gum tree, thick, opalescent, sticky dew drop diamonds; night after a storm. The garden is navy blue with the light on the other side of your skirts.

Any opiate will do, whipped or shaken, stirred or distilled, powdered or dried.

Ativan – little blue shells, little blue darlings. Capsules flood blue love into the veins. Eyes dilate, relapse, lower, and so in control, alcoholic, did we so want to survive?
Quiet, so quiet, can we endure what there is of life – the life process? The inhale, the exhale of the cigarettes. sudden deprivation of oxygen to the brain. Lips drawn in laughter. The oh, oh so feverish, four in the morning.

Crow's feet, crumbling decay. The structure folds.

With a cigarette I separate myself from "this corpse", my body. Nicotine dualism. Mind watches body with a wry humour, a disgust for flesh, drying it to the bone. Body moves from bed in the morning. Like the nicotine cloud I drift, watching the slow movements of my stiff legs, hearing their calcium click, stumbling, filling the kettle for coffee. Routine, all only routine.

The oh, oh, so routine moon landing, waking to a
world in which we subsist. World nicotine, world
word, world mind.

So hard to think, so insecure, so afraid of falling.

Alcohol bomb my brain – gin, anything to excess,
mother's ruin colourless.

Freesia petals stain my wrists, crimson drops.

After that I built my ego, slapped it on with both
hands, palmfuls of brown clay. I took a photograph, a
cigarette in the corner of the mouth, gelled hair, one
curling eyebrow.
Tape recordings borrowed from old films.

November 29th 1983

(For my good and bad angels – perhaps interchangeable)

Ursula has found her intermittent but ever constant
Birkin.
Gudrun has now gone one stage further than Gerald
and back again,
since the executioner, at the last moment, was
overcome with compassion.
You wanted to kill me and I wanted to die.
Nothing could have come between us but the law
courts.

I think it may now be too late.

I have lain beneath your dark shadow.
I have covered your black hair
with my black soul.
I am not surprised your eyes were confused
when mine were saying "kill me, kill me!"
Between your emptiness and mine there was not the
usual rift.

I think it may now be too late.

Manichea

On this beach
I have lain like a cormorant
while Raphael fought
the Witch of Endor for me.

Agnes chants in solemn round
a band of garlic on her throat.
In the dark the candles flicker.
I have lain here all my life,
in the edge of this black and white sea,
while the Devil fights for me
and God watches.

The blue eyes of God are everywhere;
infinite transcendent blue
looks back at me.
I have stared into the sky,
looked deep into your eye
and never found you watching;
for you do not lift a finger
and your thunder cannot reach me.

Opposites coexist
in mutual dependence,
moon's light reflected from the sun
and so I have thought of the Devil sometime
as your mere shadow.

Along the floor the cockroach creeps
and would climb into the flame.

I have lost a bag of images.

I have lost the types and tokens of your love.
I have dragged you everywhere with me,
in heart,
like a lead weight which kept me to the groundswell of
this ocean
like the buoy of cork which let me break the surface.
And now you are free,
and so am I.

I have lost a cluster of stars.
I have lost a hailstorm.
I have lost the edge of your lips,
fathom of your eyes,
blue horizon,
sea and sky.
Tidal wave.

Cherry Pie and Other Poems
Poems 1985–2013

Letting Go

The past can't be thrown out
so easily as these
papers and old clothes.
Instead, it waits somewhere,

like weight loss,
for its chance to return;
bringing its burden,
like lost luggage

that finally turns up
at the airport
once we have learnt at last
to live without it.

Primary Colours

I have fallen asleep on the train.
Beside me a door is ajar;
a white painted, four panelled door
with a round crazed china handle.
It is the door to the past.

I spill out into the countryside
with my suitcase of memories.

I dress myself in green.
I am young and truculent.
I think I know it all.
I don't want to listen.

I dress myself in blue.
I am true to something.
There is still something
it seems worth holding on to.

I dress myself in red.
I am a gash in the landscape.
You see me before I see you:
you get the better of me.

I dress myself in yellow.
I do not know myself.
I am not one thing or another.
I am somewhere in between.

Sleepover

My head is a cleaved coconut.
Thoughts unravel like a jumper
being undone for another;
brains becoming unstitched, spilling
loose grey jelly into the space
between action and volition;

a kind of violence to the self
that could have been stopped by sleep;
sleep that remained just out of reach
until the dawn came stealing, warm
fingered, and carried me away,
wrapped me close, but not for long.

Dreaming

If I dreamed myself
in a long night without waking,
I could walk through walls.

I could take myself to the limits
of experience, with no fear.

I could sip cocktails, naked,
on dark afternoons,
with all the lights on
and the curtains open.

The Beginning

Like a cat,
stretching and dreaming in the sun,
I bask in the warmth of your love,
luxuriate in smiles.

I wake to the morning of your love
and greet your love with mine,
in the endless succession of tomorrows
where love walks hand in hand with love.

The Excuse Me

When Grandmama told the story
of how she met Grandpapa,
he would open one eye to stare,
the only one he could see with.
A beam of sunlight through curtains
captured the golden flakes of dust,
like an old movie projector
spooling time back into the past.

It was an excuse me at a dance;
he the slick, dark haired stranger
who stepped into the circle she made
with her now unknown partner,
clasped her slim, silk clad waist to him
and with her arm on his shoulder,
whispered his promises in her ear,
spun her away into the waltz.

He would wait for her he said next
night, outside the door of the church.
So, she waited, no Grandpapa,
until after the clock had tripped
over itself twice and twice struck.
Only then she recalled, two doors
to the church, hurried back to find
him waiting at the other door.

Extreme Cold Weather

You greet me with lips of chill.
Your smile travels from Antarctica.
We have shovelled snow and eaten
the corpses of our last relationship.
What now?

A wasteland lies between us.
A transatlantic divide opens up.
Even the warmth of our lovemaking
cannot melt the ice around your heart.

Love atrophies. Even a stronger plant
might not withstand a change of climate.

Love Liberated

Yes, I do want to be
wrapped in your love,
like a warm mohair jumper;
hot love, steaming even
in the rain.

How comfortable
to snuggle back again
and glow, like an amulet
in my place
close to your heart.

But I have faced
the forest of my fears,
grown used to solitude,
learnt to stand alone,
sought out the company
of friends and books
and cannot tread the path
back to the pen.

Midnight Caress

A sudden spring thaw
came last night
to these mountains
and I beheld you
milk-faced and soft again
as a new born lamb;
the lamb that I had shepherded
and worried for so long;
the lamb and the lion
who led me
from the frowsy fug
of despair
to where he danced
in sunlight.

We licked and nuzzled.
These midnight moments,
more precious than jewels,
wrapped fast
in the scarf of memory,
sweeter than honey,
more fragile than porcelain.

The Life Laundry

They arrive early,
as the sun is up,
this man and this woman
with a purpose.

Once the dew has dried
we lay out my life
on the blameless grass;
from big hats to shoes,

so many jackets,
dresses, coats, odd socks;
so many dead guises
of my former selves;

so much sticky angst,
heavy like treacle,
is spooned into tins
and then pressed down tight.

Surplus memories,
like old frayed lampshades
or empty birdcages
flap loose in the wind.

These two sift and sort,
persuade me to sell,
to save or to shred,
to bin or to burn.

When the sun is high,
my soul, like a kite,
earthbound on its string,
shudders and tugs free.

Friday Night

Your ears dripped
gold, grapes, baubles;
your hair an exotic
coiled edifice,
treacle dark.

You leaned over me
and breathed
fantastical tales;
of ballrooms, dresses, dances,
plays and players,
dinners and delights.

In bed I would wait for you;
a rustle of satin and striped stole,
a burst of perfume and a cool breeze
from the summer garden.

You perched for a moment only,
like a tropical bird,
held my hand
and spoke;
spinning stories
of a magical world
I longed to grow up into
but have found to be
no more than a mirage,
a web of words.

Love's Improvement

Love made us so much more;
dressed us in Sunday clothes,
pinched our cheeks,
shone our shoes,
rounded out our vowels,
cured our woes.

How splendid were we?
Fine as bone china,
smoky as lapsang souchong,
sweet as honey cake,
sharp as lemons,
better than our best selves.

Tragedy

First her nose
fell off
in the shower.
She tried
to catch it
with her big toe,
but it swirled
and whirled
away from her.

All those olfactory
senses gone,
whoosh,
down the plughole
forever.

Now she couldn't
smell the flowers
in her garden
or the toast
burning,
or her husband's
sour breath.

Next her bum
slipped down the pan
while she was
doing the crossword
during a heavy session.

She knew she wouldn't
miss it.

It always looked
big in everything,
let her down really
when you came to think
about it.
Better off without a bum:
lighter altogether now.

She did miss her feet,
swept away
when she mopped the floor,
just kind of melted
somehow into the linoleum.

Now she couldn't
walk or run, or dance
or point her toes
or paint her toenails.

O well.

And then her hand
came off clean
in the tea towel
while she was
drying the dishes.

So, bit by bit
she gradually
went missing,
until in the space
of a week
she was gone.

Nothing left
but a wedding ring
and a puddle
on the floor
and a pile of empty
clothes.

It never rains
but it pours.

Dad

Dad,
this isn't the time to say goodbye,
but I am saying it every day.

I want to say:
"Hello, hello.
come in, come back.
Do not swim so far out to sea.
It's cold out there,
and we want you here,
here in the familial circle
of mirth and cheer,
of meat and wine
and summer sun,
of wit and sense
and love of life.

"Hold on,
we are coming."

RED

Red,
Promiscuous,
Lipstick,
Loose lipped,
Swinging hipped,
Thrusting, lusting,
Iridescent,
Startling,
Look at me,
No buts about it, Red.

Red,
Flame red,
Sacred pure red.

Christmas
Poinsettia red,
Cheap Santa Claus red.

Traffic light,
Sealing wax,
Official,
Stop, Go,
Yes, No,
Here now red.

Bordelais

Three hundred years ago
he was young and brown
and full of wine.
His apparel was fantastic;
the curlicues of his high hair,
the portico of his frock coat,
the elegant step of his shoe,
all brown.

He sang and danced
and entertained.
He forgot sugar and slavery.
All Europe came to see him;
to admire the proportion of his limbs,
the circulation of his blood,
to raise a toast in his wine.

Time blackened and lined his face.
His glory obscured, he was old
but full of character,
unkempt, dishevelled,
even smelly.
Yet still he drew the crowds.

They put him under a tap
and scrubbed at him
till he came out clean.

Still his cold, stony skin
had the sad fragrance
of better days.
His breath was coffee and garlic.

His clothes reeked of petrol,
of cigarettes and backstreets,
redolent of memories;
of fountains and muses,
of backstairs and boulevards,
of servants' quarters,
and ladies' chambers,
of the theatre and the bar
and the docks.

Three hundred years ago
he was young and brown
and full of wine.

The Battle of the Fell

From my window I am watching the Indians,
brave souls rooted against a smoky sky.
A dozen or so stark, lonely firs
seem to be making a stand for freedom,
behind them drifting cloud, fading sunlight.
The cowboys are all in the valley.
Tension. I wait for the fight to break out,
for the frown of the skyline to buckle down
to the valley floor with its fast flowing
river, its rocks and its rapids and roads.
instead, the equilibrium holds:
the earth continues its eternal round.

Our Marriage:

wears like a baggy jumper,
reassuringly warm in winter,
out at the elbows after ten years,
room enough for three.

thrills like a silk dress,
irradiates the skin.
It sometimes feels like
wearing nothing at all.

like our Levi jeans
conveys respect for equals,
two original thinkers
growing old together.

like a pair of kinky cuffs
locks me to you
and you to me,
for as long as we are pleased to let it.

In this three-legged race
neither one can run fast
and many times we fall down and cry,
but we've got each other.

When My Father Died

"He's already cold," my mother said.
I bent and kissed his cooling brow,
still warm to me after the starry chill
of the December night I shrugged
off with my coat, still warm like fresh bread.

I saw that his eyes, those eyes
that had tracked me only hours before
now followed nothing,
but were otherwise the same.

I had met those quick brown eyes
and I had known, that whatever
was left unsaid would never now be said.

I was saying goodbye, and so I had
just said "I love you," not knowing
if he would need such information;
or even if he heard me or knew
anything beyond the pain of the infection
that would stop his heart.

And so I said goodbye again, moments
before they came and scooped him up
like a broken toy, in his striped, boy blue
pyjamas and zipped him up in a black bag,
right over the head.

I wondered how he would breathe now.
For days I lay awake at night,
worrying that he would be cold
with no one to warm his bones,
not accepting that he was dead
and beyond any further hurt.

Dead, dead, my father dead;
her husband dead.

No other word could fill our mouths
for days, as if we had to make it true,
and still it astonished.

Preludes

A little rain
absolves us of these feelings.

Can we find the heart
to love again;
unfold like flowers,
open faces, hands,
to a wet kissing sky?

Rain like punctuation,
slanted commas
in a grey street;
the rain falls between
and between,
washing out endings
or beginnings.

Rain and wind
reach a crescendo,
almost drown out
the orchestra
playing in the cathedral.

The music climbs,
grows louder,
plays out its own storm,
begins, ends,
begins again.

Heavy rain.
We walk home
arm in arm,
sharing one umbrella.

Gloves

In winter,
gloves graced her outfit;
either worn or carried,
like a posy of fingers
in one hand.

Gloves were her entrance cards.
She was a member
of the club.

She belonged to the town:
she knew what she owed.
Respect was mutual:
the town loved her back.

Soft leather
belied
washing up hands,
thick cables of veins,
knotty joints;
the years of rubbing fat into flour.

Other Lives

In the mirror I am left-handed:
I read from the back to the front.
In these lines is written
the story of my life.

In the mirror other lives were possible.
In the mirror I have lived
there, where you always
loved me.

In the mirror I embrace
the dead in my own image:
with these eyes they return
my gaze.

In the mirror I am given
back to myself.
in the mirror
I might be someone else.

From the other side,
the other self reaches out
one silver backed hand
and pulls me through.

Sea Stones

These stones:
rolled in the maw of the sea,
rounded with tough love,
gathered from all the beaches
I have visited in a while now;
I like to hold them
and remember
sunlit sands,
and endless evenings
of never wanting to leave,
but hold onto the moment,
make a fist around it,
hard as a stone.

Sacrifice

Late at night,
when the windowpane turns black,
come the summer brides,
sad soft bodies
in tobacco brown dresses;
and straight away they want out.

This glare was not the one they wanted:
they wanted the moon.

Shimmy up the glass
in a blur of wings,
fall into water
and stick like petals,
cannot be lifted
and even if dried
will die;
they putter out their
brief lives
while I watch.

Like Whisky, Like Honey

When you go,
if you must go,
leave me only your voice,
like whisky, like honey;
a warm burr
in the ear,
like the bees
busy in your flower garden
on long summer Sundays
with newspapers
and tea and cakes.

When you go,
if you must go,
leave me only your voice,
like whisky, like honey,
the silky thrill
of an indecent proposition.

The Meaning of Home

The place knows you,
comes forward to meet you,
rubs itself against your shins.

Everything is familiar;
the stones worn by your feet
and the feet of those you love,

the kettle on the hob,
the robe behind the door,
the books on the table.

There may be music
or the chatter of conversation
or the quietness and cool of a cloister.

Here you can empty yourself out.
Here you can be filled up again
and sent out into the world.

Here you may always return
and never be found wanting.
Here you will always belong.

Our Anniversary: An Oyster Bar

In the moment of swallowing,
sliding gelatinously over the throat,
leaving a trace of the elusive taste,
neutral, indefinable,
the oyster is gone:
becomes yesterday's oyster.

I photograph you mid slurp;
freeze the moment, stop time.

The oyster man splits open more oysters.
Another couple shuffles in under the tarpaulin
and huddles from the spooling rain.
The oyster woman slicks her hands down her apron
and takes another order.

In our mind's eye
the pale gleam of a briny pearl,
never formed;
twenty-three years of prising ourselves apart.

Family Christmas

It is the close of Christmas Day.
The four of us, all that are left,
are at table, loaded with cold
meat and pickles, wine in our glasses.

The Angel chimes won't go around,
so we give them a helping hand.
There is space between our shoulders,
large gaps where others can get in.

We feel that we are not alone:
the dead sit down and eat with us,
pass the salt and pull the crackers.
Every year, they are always here.

Their mirth, the joy of Christmas past,
shadows our fragile enjoyment.
It will not leave us to ourselves,
but pulls us back to be with them.

Cherry Pie

We planted a morello cherry tree.
For three years we let it fruit untouched.
We found the glut to be picked off by birds;
then learnt to beat them to the crimson hoard.

Before this rain, there were years of plenty.
You persevered to stone all the cherries,
baked them in pies. Some we kept for ourselves
and still, we had enough to give away.

Once your chain saw pruning was so brutal
I expected nothing more from the tree.
It came back stronger still. You baked more pies.
We ate and ate. A taste so sweet and tart.

Meditation in Summer

Here now.
No here.
But here now.
The blue tit's splash
of blue and yellow
alights on each of three
fence panels in turn,
puffs out his tiny portent,
and is gone.

I look up into
the leaves of the horse chestnut,
falling down over me.
A lit green canopy
envelops me. light enters me,
illumines me from within.

Inside I am blue,
or green, or blue,
a trembling leaf on
a tree or the surface
of an electric lake.

Racing in My Sleep

He's way up ahead already,
just a streak on the horizon.
I want to keep him in my sights
but I am still tying my laces;

and then they tell me he's long gone.
I'll be lucky if I catch him,
since he was always laps ahead,
knew what he wanted, went for it.

It's then I see the road in front
of me, veering up to the sky;
narrow and steep, criss-crossed with roots
and rocks and brambles and sharp snares.

First Things

These things were always here;
long before we broke free
from Mum's wide skirts,
to run clear under tables,
around chair legs,
over lawns of daisies,
down to the apple orchard.
Always.

A cup with a lid and a fixed smile;
spoon with God enrobed on its handle;
a leering clown candlestick;
the small key in the wardrobe
which seems to turn by itself
when you almost close your eyes:
from these we construct
our map of meaning.

Poems features in the Poetry
Aloud third-year anniversary
celebration, 2011

Bringing Down the Moon

You net the moon for me,
bring it down
with an 80mm lens
to about the size of a potato.

I'm looking down
on its swarthy lustre,
can almost see
those first footsteps
falling on dreams.
Everything's so clear,
so sharp,
like stippled white emulsion.

I marvel,
imagine its weight
in the palm of my hand;
craggy ellipsis,
rugged, heavy,
luminous.

Can this be the moon?

Black cloud
like smoke
drifts across this face,
is gone.

And then
the lens dims,
thick grey cloud closes
and the light is gone.

We are alone with each other.

A Sense of Self

After all, I am not
who you take me to be,
nor who I took myself to be
a moment ago either.

Which one was it you wanted?
Selves reside here;
angry young woman lives here
and inner child
and disillusioned fifty something.

Sometimes I catch myself
looking back at me.
Sometimes I can meet
my eye. But mostly
I elude myself especially.

Myself is like the long looked for,
long dead black cat
from my childhood
appearing in the corner
of my eye, for a moment,
then gone, a trick of the light.

Being most looked for
I am most hard to find
and still don't know myself.

New Poems
2013–2022

I, Asterion

Son of my snow-white father,
from whom my strength derives,
and my soft bodied,
soft minded mother

have been trapped here
my whole life long
in this maddening
catacomb of passages.

No way out.
My hunger and my anger
know no bounds.
I cry to you:

bring me human flesh,
the sweeter
and more tender
the better.

Bring me your young
who have not yet coupled
and I will eat them up
and spit out their bones.

Copenhagen

The sky, bird's egg
blue, shields the fragility
of the day. Your fever
has ridden the night,
broken it asunder.

From the boat
the guide announces;
Hans Christian Andersen's
houses, the 'oops moment',
the Royal palace.

We eat Danish pastries,
kebabs at 'Street Food'
on Christianshavn,
the 'best cake in
Scandinavia.'

On our last morning
we absorb everything;
the winter garden
at the heart of Carlsberg
Glyptotek, the Rodin

and the Degas dancer,
stepping forward eternally
in her faded muslin.
We see it all and try
to take it with us.

Becoming Mother

A young person old age has happened to,
you come towards me with uncertain gait,
and always I see your mother in you;
the mother you hoped not to emulate.
Yet like your mother you'll stay up till three
to complete a task that could be made wait.
"You're not a finisher," you say of me.
I'm someone else another size and shape;
a taller woman of a different hue,
who has sewed a seam but chooses now instead
to make no cakes nor any Irish stew,
but cook with words, with poets break my bread.
Me to you, I'm the apple to your pear:
I can never be you and so forbear.

The Dell

Isobel took me down the dell;
down through the undergrowth
to her imaginary world.

She taught me how to suck nectar
out of white dead nettles;
so we could eat like the fairies.

She told me what sarcasm was.
She lashed out with her tongue.
Things aren't always what they seem.

We stayed up all night and cut
up a rug and stuck it under
our arms for grown-up hair.

And then we fell out.

Blackbird Divo

Feet planted on the apex of the shed roof,
the blackbird fills the green cathedral
with the sound of its song, floating
upward to the overarching trees
where it is answered by another call
further off. The blackbird is oblivious
to all else, but the song and its answering
song, the tak, tak, tak of its alarm call
filling the late afternoon, calling me down
the garden to draw back the branches
of the cherry tree and find it there,
shaking out its feathers like shards
of jet, resplendent and territorial,
the aria flowing from its bent yellow beak.

Just Married, 1987

Like cans tied to our bumper,
we are already trailing the past.
My ex-lovers and your father
come along for the ride.

Your white suit and my polka
dot dress and jaunty hat
make a show for the crowd.
There is fog at Gatwick.

We sit up all night waiting
for our flight. Our future
is a blank page we think,
flying high above clouds.

In Portugal we swim naked
in the thunderous waves,
spend nights at the jazz bar,
empty, out of season.

We drink black Russians
and dine on fresh sardines.
I cry for my past trauma
and you still dry my tears.

Gerbera

Scentless gerbera
present surprised,
designer faces,
in candy colours

to match your dress.
Each daisy wheel
a shower of petals
to tear and tell.

She loves me.
She loves not me.
She loves not.

I love her.
I love not her.
I love not.

Learning to Swim

Each small body
in its sleek suit
up
and then vertiginously
down.

I have fallen
into a ravine
with blue sides.
I may never find my way
out.

Blue fills my world,
blue and the fear
of blue,
bubbles,
limbs.

And then, unexpectedly,
I am coming up
and out,
breaking the surface
of blue.

Melanoma

All the way to the hospital
the lights stay on green. I pray too.
God speaks to each in her own voice.
He holds a mirror up to hope.

So many things that could go wrong
but didn't. Now I rehearse them.
You say when you are up against
it he is there for you, no doubt.

We wait on hard chairs for the knife.
For me there is only the still
moment of contemplation, now
that there is nothing else to do.

A Monument for Lost Things

There should be a monument for lost things;
the things people lose down the backs of chairs,
leave at the library or on the bus,
and never come back for, that disappear.
Where do they go, the lost things, the marriage
licenses, and bus tickets and wedding rings?
Do they have another life in repose,
and will they all come back to us again?
Is there a place that all the lost things go,
unreachable by us who feel their lack,
on a separate plane or ghostly sphere
subsisting in parallel with our life?
If so this monument must live among
the shades, unseen by mortal, human eyes.

Walter

After he died the first time
we found him sitting up in bed,
sheepish at all the attention,
eating sausages and cabbage.
Hospital food. St Mary's.
He never complained;
it was all better than the navy,
joining it at seventeen
because it seemed safest,
surviving the battle of Jutland.

My babysitter until fourteen;
he sat under the lamp and dozed
while I watched old movies,
Whatever Happened To Baby Jane?
and re-enactments of the First
World War – crying when they shot
deserters. "It wasn't like that,"
he called up the stairs, where
I had gone to sob my heart out.
I never asked what it was like.

After that scare he was shaky.
He seemed not quite of this world.
Learning to drive, I dreamt
each night of a car that wouldn't stop;
me at the wheel, him the passenger.
The following year in a January storm,
the aorta disconnected. My mother
arrived at the hospital to find him
pink from so much oxygen, but this
time he wasn't coming back.

Him Outdoors, Her Indoors

She is bedroom slippers.
He is steel-toe boots.
He waters, she washes.
He reaps, she sews.
He digs, she rummages.
She mops. He mows.

Him indoors, her outdoors

He's naked as he's born.
She's dressed for town.
He tidies, she walks.
She swims. He surfs.
He bakes, she talks.
He waits. She's late.

Murmuration

At each day's end there's a crowd of starlings
in our sky, ribboned across the fading light.
We watch the dance, as they fling outwards,
never losing touch, then gather in a peak
of darkness, again and again, as if held
by an invisible force. We are captivated.

In church we mumble our responses,
a little out of sync with each other,
creating a continuous babble of sound.
As we try to pray our thoughts
scatter and regroup, fly heavenward
or contract in a nub of concentration.

The audience waiting for the play
to start, raise their voices in a hubbub
of anticipation, rustle sweet wrappers
and flip through their programmes,
chatter about this and that right up
until the lights dim and the curtain rises.

Dream Tsunami

I was wearing my best boots,
feet together on the yellow
sand, hoping not to spoil
the suede, when the water rose.

Now they were getting soaked.
Suddenly the wave was all
around and then behind me,
a shock-tall wall of water,

overtopping the world.
I knew that I must plunge
through its heart, but my
chances were small to none.

The Owl

These last evenings
the dark is punctuated
by an owl.

When my mood
empties out
like a cup

drained to the leas
or brim again of life,
then drained;

the owl's cry
shivers and halloos
to me.

The call seeks
like a lighthouse
searchlight,

sweeping the distance,
and finding out
the heart of me.

The Film of Arriving Home

Outside, the squat car,
small and cat black,
pulled up into itself
like a full stop.

On the inside,
abandoned bags.
Jangle of keys
on the gramophone.

Crumbs littering
on a white plate
speak of you
but don't tell all.

The back door open,
like a question mark,
arches into light
and birdsong.

The air is sliced
by the sound of
the lawnmower.
Cut to your face.

The Fall

The girl who is young,
like the first summer,
reaches the springboard's end,
misses her footing.

Now she is a vase
falling from a ledge,
over and over
she falls flawlessly,

falls for a long time,
still whole, still beautiful;
hits the water and breaks
into a thousand pieces of light.

The Lost Library Book

The lost book waits for you,
forgotten among other books
that have been better loved;
that have known fingertips
tracing their paper, eyes
following the line of a thought,
chasing a paragraph to its
conclusion. Halt right there!

You are this book's last chance.
Check it out and it will
live in your hands, its pages
turn in accord with your desires,
its print and pictures flower
in your brain – if not it must die;
pulled to an untimely death,
pulped and gone forever.

The Silence

How you just left
without a forwarding address,
everything as if you had only
stepped out for a moment;
clothes draped on the backs of chairs,
lipsticks open on the dressing table,
washing up to be done.

No time to pack,
you took the direct route,
straight to the pearly gates.

After that I never heard
from you again.
The silence met me halfway.
No more phone conversations
where you would ring me back
two or three times to make
your point. No more flashing light
on the answerphone or calls
to my mobile at work.

I'd imagine I heard you
talking in my ear, saying
something you've said before,
but it was only the static
singing in the trees.
The silence was absolute,
cavernous, unbroken.
It took up residence.

Helenium

Named for Helen of Troy,
daughter of Zeus and Leda,
she whose radiant beauty
surpassing all others

unleashed Ares, god of war,
and set city state against
city state when Menelaus'
wrath pursued Paris,

Helenium, turns its bright
daisy wheel of burnt orange
petals to the sun and showers
of late summer and autumn,

lending its flame to light
us towards winter, leading
us by the hand in the growing
dark of the equinox.

Migraine

First came the euphoria,
the manic impulses,
the craving for oranges.
Then - after I had devoured
the bright fruit - the slipped
stitch, whirling crab,
watery hole in the fabric
of things, expanded
until it could swallow
houses, continents.

It took out whole eyes,
mine in the mirror.
Now we were all Cyclopes.
Heads were sheared off
like jagged eggshells.
The time hid from me,
numerals and hands
coming and going
in a cruel game
of hide and seek.

Like a sheet of paper
torn down the middle
language was severed from
meaning. I lay in the dark
and tried to name familiar
things, but nothing came.
A pulse kept time to
the drumbeat in my head,
that threatened to engulf me,
then, with a last roll, ceased.

Coffee and Radio

Weak, citrus sunlight gleams in the window
where white chrysanthemums stand still.

Apples stay put in their bowl, smile knowingly,
as bananas stretch cramped fingers towards
some question not yet asked.

'*Saturday Live*' is the accompaniment
to our shared breakfast. Coffee filters
as croissants crisp in the oven.

We have not yet touched the lip of the day.

The Witchfinder General

*In August 1645, two hundred witches were tried
at Bury St Edmunds: 124 presented to the court by
Matthew Hopkins. It has been suggested in a number
of books that 68 of these were hanged, though this is
probably a bit of an exaggeration. (From* Witches In
and Around Suffolk, *by Pip and Joy Wright, 2004)*

If she's lighter than the bible,
if she be wise beyond your ken,
and if her imp can find lost things;
swim her then.

If she the future can divine,
if she has herbs to cool your brow,
and if her look blight you or yours;
swim her now.

If holy water spit her out
and she stand then upon dry land;
prevail on her till she confess.
She will hang.

The Poet Has Compassion for Herself

Give her a break
why don't you?
She's always here
to answer your call

twenty-four seven,
come rain or shine,
in sickness and in health,
till death you do part.

She does her best for you,
pushes you onwards,
helps you pick yourself up
when you are down.

Where do you think
your strength comes from
if not from her and she
will always be here?

She will always be here
and if you let her
she will always love you,
always treat you with kindness.

Just like you she didn't
live up to expectations,
but like you she is good
enough, "as good as gold."

Upon Looking at a Wine-Jar in the British Museum.

Museum number
1836,0224.127

Here on a Grecian wine-jar
Achilles confronts Penthesilea,
Amazon, warrior queen.

Where is her strength
as she crumples on one knee,
her spear missing its mark?

Achilles is all magnificent limbs
and black armour, while she
exposes her face and throat

and I realise when I see
the spurt of red blood
from her jugular

that this is the moment
when her life
rushes out

and Achilles,
it is said,
falls in love.

*Black-figured amphora (wine-jar), made in Attica,
Greece, 530-525 BC.*

In the Cleft of the Tree

And still my youthful mind belies my age;
how long my gawky greening days are done.
I hide behind rough bark that is my face.

I ask myself should I grow old with grace;
or would a girlish recklessness be wrong?
And still my youthful mind belies my age.

Should I wear red with purple at this stage,
disport myself in town and have some fun?
I hide behind rough bark that is my face.

I'd rather give the morning greater place
than pay my homage to a ghosted moon.
Yet still my youthful mind belies my age.

From inside out it can be hard to gauge
just how another person will see one.
I hide behind rough bark that is my face.

These numbers are a thing I can't embrace;
how easily I am outpaced, outshone.
And still my youthful mind belies my age;
I hide behind rough bark that is my face.

Home

As I turn the corner,
the curve of our street
and in the crook of its arm
our house, with the yellow door.

Inside a riot of things;
books and papers and tools,
fills the space and overflows
into the future.

Good times: pancakes
and parties, candles and company;
in summer the garden, ripe
with raspberries and redcurrants.

In a winter such as this
I look for a light, signalling
that you are there before me;
for you are home to me.

Squishy Squashy

The twilight darkens like a bruise;
velvet with a sheen of longing.

On the plum tree by the window
the purple fruit are ripe and split.

Instead of picking them to eat
my nine-year-old niece places them

in the road and scarpers.
Cars that emerge like shadows

swoop out of growing darkness
and spatter them under tyres,

while she stays safe and whole
behind the small white painted gate.

Squishy squashy.

The Weeping Birch

The weeping
birch shakes out its
silver-green skirts in the April
breeze, fluttering its tiny, tinsel
heart in such a shy way, it might
make me think it had something to hide
behind its shimmering curtain of bright,
shiny leaves. Oh, weeping birch,
weep for me. My eyes
have been dry these four-
teen long years and who
knows what sorrow

I	am
h	iding
in	my
h	eart?

Ode to Olive Oil

The olive
grows
tenaciously
and just as vigorously
in Israel as in Palestine;
on sun-baked,
arid terraces
climbing to the sky.
Its first virginal
pressing,
green and cool
as hidden,
deep-clouded,
lilied ponds.
Will you marry it,
love it,
drown in it,
drink it,
cook with it?
A plate of lentils
and fennel;
simple ascetic food.
Or cascade it
down his back,
worked warmly
into the hands,
as fingers search
out the knots
and find their way
home?

Tinker, Tailor

After we ate the plums
we girls counted the stones,
lining them up on the edge
of the dish with a spoon.

Tinker, tailor, soldier, sailor.
Not what I would grow up
to be, but who I would marry.
Why was it always soldier?

Not a lot of choice perhaps.
I dreaded those lunches,
often kept back to eat
the horrible spotted dick.

My Mother's Story

My mother stands
at the edge of the group
of eleven young women;
delirious smile, dark hair
abundant under the white
cook's hat. Arms behind
her back she leans slightly
forwards, a stance familiar
from later years.

How she got there:
a story she told and told,
her road to glory,
the only girl in physics.
She had to have a science,
saw the headmaster,
got her way. A decision made
at eleven, copying a neighbour
with a car she coveted.

She loved her subject,
faced many challenges,
tea for four hundred
being one of the first.
She's eighteen in nineteen
fifty, not even dreaming
of me. Once established,
a domestic science teacher,
then she meets my father.

In Lockdown

The fourth week of lockdown
and we are both still here;
you in work, facing the world;
me at home, embracing solitude.

We have survived so much else.
Now we all face the same fear,
the same drowning in air
for want of oxygen.

Yet here is April sunshine.
I sit alone under the umbrella
at the familiar, slate picnic table
and read books I have never

had time to read and drain
my black tea to the last drop.
Every day of virus free existence
is a day reclaimed from the void.

For fear of infection, we ration
our kisses, then kiss in a fervour
defying the fates. Let us not
part at last un-kissed.

How to Sing if You are Bad

Firstly, sit or stand upright,
inclining neither to right nor left.
Learn to breathe
from the earth's core.
Let the vowels escape
your open mouth,
flat as feet, as dragged down
by their own weight,
they fall on the unsuspecting.

Tilt your chin down
like a rangefinder
and now forage higher
or lower, roaming where
you should never be.

Be all head or all heart,
or somewhere in between.

Drink water.

Practice every day.
Become a hummer.
Haunt the shower
and the karaoke.

In the music room,
Miss Struthers' slingbacks
fraternise on the pedals
of the piano. "Just sing your
favourite hymn." You carol
from the depths of your nine-
year-old frame, maltesers

and string in your pockets.
"Praise my soul the King of…"
The teacher eyes you earnestly.
"Come again whenever you like,"
she says when your voice squalls.

Window

Window in winter;
the sad, grimy glass
allowing light while
shielding us from cold.
Still one or two dead
flies, casualties from
the summer, transfixed
in spider's web veils
on the dusty sill.

Window in summer;
open, beckoning us
from this small space
to the great outside.
Life is to be lived on
a larger canvas; wide
blue sky, birds flying,
a breeze blowing us
into our tomorrow.

Window with flowers.
A set piece. The frame
is all. Overblown lilies
shed papery petals,
leak ginger pollen,
like a season starting
to be over. A three
legged art deco jug
completes the picture.

A Chant Against Loneliness in Lockdown

After Mervyn Morris

Say shout across the distance.
Say wave through a closed window.
Say I hug me
and you hug you.

Say radio.
Say phone-ins.
Say Zoom
I'm in your living room.

Say poetry
your quiet friend.
Say animals
who understand.

Say solo cycle rides
or bracing walks.
Say telephones
for soulful talks.

Say the sun in the morning,
the moon and stars at night.
Say love is still out there
to make it right.

The Monster in the Mirror

When I look at myself
cold in the morning
the monster's sister
looks right back.

These hazel eyes
I got them from my father.
I have been stitched
together from the dead.

But I have drunk the wine,
drunk it down and put
the stopper back in the bottle.
None shall come after me
to see their make-up
in the mirror.
It all ends here.

If every mind event
is a brain event
then I'm here
behind the eyes.

Sometimes I leap
into the realisation
like a big cat.

If I didn't know this
I would think I lived
further down; somewhere
more low-slung, the pelvis
perhaps, or behind the heart,
where it hurts.

just one breath

for the early wakening

just one breath
for all our loss

just one breath
for the ins and outs
of a conflicted life

just one breath
for the rising panic
which grips and
doesn't let go

just one breath

Felixstowe Reprised

A timid sea sparkles like diamonds
under a cotton clouded sky.
When we find a shop with a welcome,
we raid it for kitchenware and gifts.
A table outside an Italian restaurant,
the only one open on the seafront.
I order seafood soup and ravioli.
I can taste the risk. The glare so bright
I'm missing sunglasses I don't own.
An unmasked woman comes too close:
"I had the meatballs, very filling.
Take my tip and have the meatballs
next time." We go in search of ice-cream,
lick and drip our way along the prom.

Reunion: *Aberystwyth*

September, yet the heat Mediterranean,
the setting sun gilding the sea: we waited
to meet old friends.

A sideways look over his pint: "what've you
been doing for the last thirty-four years?"
I tried to fill him in.

Rinsing these thoughts through, the sea below
kept me from sleep, its slow sighing breaths
never in time with mine.

High up at Cwrt Mawr, she and I saw families
disgorging their clear-eyed offspring
from their four by fours.

Children from a wedding, tiny in suits and frocks,
played around the columns of the National Library.
Sheep huddled in front.

Tripping down stone steps to Gwesty Cymru,
we ate under pink lighting; till she and I cut loose
and kicked the bar.

Now it was the students and the seagulls
that kept it up till three a.m.
Was this once us?

Up the zigzag gravel path on Constitution Hill
I struggled for breath. Unsure of my footing
on the rocky summit.

Turning at last, we saw the bay unroll beneath us,
sudden like a gifted bolt of bright, blue silk;
sun on the slate roofed town.

I looked down on Alexandra Hall, our seafront
residence, and could conjure myself pacing
as I read the Iliad.

From bed to window and back again;
limber and sure of everything then:
I had left a part of myself here.

We descended the hill and caught our train.
At New Street we parted. It won't be thirty-four years
before I'm back.

The Grandfather Clock

Not a shy tick tock
but an insistent,
judgemental sound,
that filled the otherwise
cold and silent hallway;
with the small fridge
made to look like
a hard wood cabinet
and the umbrella stand.

An early nineteenth century
mahogany long case clock,
it kept me from sleep
those nights in the bedroom
at Grandma and Grandpa's;
where I could see my breath
as I lay stiffly between sheets
which had been lately heated
by the copper warming pan.

If I made it through the night
the morning brought such
pleasures as chipolatas,
porridge, toast and marmalade.
All was warm and light,
sitting at the yellow Formica
table with the two of them,
long, black vanilla pods
in the jars of sugar.

In later years, Grandma gone,
and the bungalow broken up,
the clock stood in a corner
at seventeen, where its noise
could not find me upstairs;
and it would sometimes fall
silent until it was wound.

The Year's Midnight

A pale sun struggles to come through the fog.
There are frosted rosebuds in the rose garden,
yew trees and ruins in mist. Tropical birds
still dance and touch beaks in their cages.

A string of light bulbs adorns the fruit and veg stall.
They tell me how everything is constantly sanitised.
I buy blueberries, lemons and limes for the evening.
My hands gripping the bag are crippled with cold.

The virus draws its net tighter, yet out of fear
and despair can come hope. We will walk
these streets again and we will kiss and hug.
Skin will know skin.

Plongeuse

(Plongeuse is a French word used to describe a person washing up in a restaurant, but it can also mean an underwater diver.)

It's the early eighties
and I'm washing up
in a hotel in France.

There's a bus strike on
and I've borrowed a bicycle
to get to work.

It's only a temporary job
to cover for sick leave,
but I can dream.

I pull on the yellow
rubber gloves, turn on the tap
and squeeze in the detergent.

I grab a stack of plates
and get started, my hands
sinking into the suds,

getting a rhythm going,
leaning forward a bit too much,
my feet leave the floor.

I'm plunging head over heels
into the bowl and down and out
the other side into the ocean.

The rubber gloves have gone
and my body is now encased
in a sleek black wetsuit.

There is an aqualung
on my back, a light on my head.
I see all the wonders of marine life

go by: a walrus, dolphins, turtles,
tuna, a manatee and rays
as I go deeper and deeper.

Great white sharks circle me,
sea horses hang suspended
below me with bony perfection.

All sense of time has gone.
So too has the hotel,
the restaurant, the customers

waiting for clean plates,
the kind friend waiting for her
bicycle, and I am here,

an astronaut whirling
in space, going deeper,
finally touching down

and walking on the ocean
floor. Now I have something
to write home about.

Birch Trees

The cherry tree,
savaged previously
with a chainsaw,
was a casualty
because it interfered
with the weeping birch,
planted for your birthday;
and the silver birch
at the end of the garden,
planted to replace
the eucalyptus
which toppled
in high winds
and took four of us
to bring down finally,
grows and grows
towards heaven,
where only the birds
can reach, and sways
precariously in the breeze.

The Lockdown Day

Each morning waking in darkness
with darkness in my heart,
until I shake the shadows free
in the shower, go downstairs
and make strong coffee, switch
on '*Today*' and life begins.

Locked down together,
tea and cake in the afternoons,
also weather that squalls and shines
like old coins made new,
as winter recedes and spring
is slow in coming.

Sally

from the Hebrew;
a diminutive of Sarah,
meaning princess.

Sally, clean cut, fifties
blond; girl next door.
she's feisty, doesn't give
up easily. You know she
won't let you down.

'Mustang Sally,'
'Long tall Sally,'
'Pride of our alley;'
you're one hard
act to follow.

Urban Walking

Out and free but for the mask,
moving through air with unrestricted steps,
getting into my stride, a measure the Fitbit
can comprehend, half the incentive of being here.
My feet striking pavement then tarmac,
I step into the road, avoiding others
I might have been happy to greet,
keeping a wide berth and moving on.
Looking for something I haven't seen before;
a poster in a window near the YMCA.
In bright pink it arrests my attention.
Crossing the street. "Keep Yer Chin Up Again."
A sun breaking through, molten behind the mist,
snowdrops in snow, resilient with antifreeze,
golden celandines, no fish in the pond
nor ducks on the water.

Like Mother, Like Daughter

It was the night I pushed
the small, pink, varnished shell
up my nose that my mother
gave me her doll. I'd never
seen it before and I held on
to it as we drove through
the dark streets to the surgery
where the doctor used forceps
to extract the obstructing carapace
that clattered in the steel dish.

Later I learned that my mother
had done the same thing at a
similar age with a puzzle piece.
It was the highlight of my father's
lauded speech at our wedding;
how my husband was marrying
into a dynasty of women who
shoved things up their noses.

My mother and I held hands
at the top table. She said:
"Will you kill him, or shall I?"

Shoes

that gather in groups
and then disperse,
that are never in the room
where you left them.

Shoes that become familiar,
that cleave to your feet,
bear you up,
take you all over the city.

New shoes that know
no mercy, inflict pain
like no other. Will you walk
again in these shoes?

Shoes that speak
of love or status
ballet shoes or patent leather,
knee high boots.

How I loved

my father's typewriter
from the nineteen forties
that sat up straight
on the dining room table

with its round lozenges
of keys and how you knew
if you wrote too fast
they would all jam.

The satisfying clunk
of each stroke
as you fell into rhythm,
the thrill of carriage return.

The way you could insert
a blank sheet of paper
wind it in, type your title,
think you were Hemingway.

The Grey Lady of Bury St Edmunds

On a cold, misty afternoon in January
I trek, solitary as a shade, from haunt
to haunt on the trail of the Grey Lady.

At the West Front I ask myself
should I knock loudly on a door
since her footsteps might approach
but never arrive?

I pass through the throng in Abbeygate
Street. Here the Grey lady clicked
her heels on carpet in a ladies' outfitters
and walked through the wall.

I come to Cupola House, where she
is said to have haunted the cellar,
to St Saviour's Hospital, helping troubled souls
since the reign of King John,

where she appeared and was gone
almost as soon as she was seen
and lastly Fornham Priory, where she
leapt the wall.

And so, homeward, a grey lady myself,
fading from sight like the apparition,
vanishing from society, a woman
of a certain age.

The Invitation

Let's go Greek,
share a mezze platter
and tiny coffees with grounds
at the bottom.

Shall we sit in the small café
at a table very close
to the next one,
fall into conversation

with our neighbours
and watch the people
passing on the pavement
without a care?

The Clear Out

You say you feel
like a child
facing a tsunami

and I picture you
on the beach,
immobilised,

the moment before
the water reaches
the shore

and takes you with it;
and I pray that you
find something

inside yourself,
some way forward,
that lets you tackle

the wall of things
overwhelming your world
and take it out

piece by piece
and bring it safely
down to earth.

Rain Comes to Norwich

Rain sluices the plate glass window of the café.
We have taken off our dripping coats,
but are wet through. There are good luck cards
on a table and I sense this is a new venture;
brownies and coffee; 'yes to brownies;'
all the brownies you might want or imagine.
We have found our refuge from the shower,
heavy and prolonged. We sip tea from small cups,
happy not to be outside as a man sprints across
the market place, ankle deep in the deluge.
Your disappointment sits between us like a reproach.
The one day out and the exhibition a let-down,
the restaurant not open, photography shop closed.
The rain dissipates. We buy brownies to go,
and leave laden with shopping to get fish and chips
in Goat Lane and so we give up and go home.

Clavicle

A hockey or a hurling stick,
a long, curved, horizontal bone
from shoulder blade to sternum;

like being let into a secret,
what appears above the neckline
hints at more.

Small key, bar or bolt
a tendril, clasper, cirrus,
young shoot of creeping plant;

fragile as a flower,
sophisticated as darjeeling,
playing its song on a clavichord.

The End of Summer

The lasting image of the day
is a child, a wisp of a thing,
no more than three years old,
in pink, who plays with the sea.

She runs and stamps her boot
and back to mum who waits.
The sea sends out its tongue
over the wet sand to trick her.

Each moment I wait for her
to be overwhelmed, but
the girl is quick and she
gets away again and again.

The day is ending. The tide
is going out as the sun sinks
landward over the pier
and at last, she runs away.

Retirement Deferred

Retirement was on the horizon;

a vista of sunlit streets,
of writing on my laptop in cafes,
of walking where my feet took me
instead of rushing home with groceries.

I could read too, all those books
in teetering piles beside my bed,
instead of just in borrowed moments
in lunch hours or between chores.

I imagined sorting all my papers,
opening all my post directly,
a clean, well-run house,
no more unhealthy, late suppers.

Or simply leisure, the time
to get things done or just to be.

And then it wasn't happening after all.
The horizon just got further away.

Abiding Love

In a dark time, you bring home a flower,
"Celica deep orange," Celica from the Latin
coelica, meaning heavenly or celestial.

On two tall stems, grow big, flame coloured
blooms, each a four trumpeted heart,
glowing, seemingly rare or divine.

This beauty, more rarefied than our earthly,
human love, lasts for day upon day,
greets us each morning with new grace.

For we know now, you and I, that our love
has not only lasted but will endure
and outlast the storms to come.

Acknowledgements

This collection couldn't have come about without the help and support of many other people, to name a few: everyone at Poetry Aloud (especially Rob Lock, Jen Overett, Colin Whyles, Derek Adams, Richard Whiting, Ian Speed, Kaaren Whitney, Joe Thraveson-Lambert and Martin Hayden), The Arvon Foundation, Catherine Terry, Fraser Harrison, Diana Banks, Denise James Van Camp, Lindsay Smith, David Rogers, and all at Kingston University Press (notably Emma Tait, Amanda Carungi, Ashmi Bhatt, Ben Tickner, Georgina Dent and Jasmine Higgins) and my husband, William McDonald.

Credits

'A Chant Against Loneliness in Lockdown' (page 100) first published on *Bury Free Press* community page, 5th June 2020.

'Coffee and Radio' (page 85) first published in *Twelve Rivers* Volume 10 Issue 1, 2019.

'The Monster in the Mirror' (page 101) first published by *Ink Sweat & Tears*.

'Window' (page 99) first published by *@Ease Magazine*, March 2018.

Thanks to Pip Wright for permission to reproduce text from his book *Witches In and Around Suffolk* (Pawprint Publishing, 2004) on page 86.

Lightning Source UK Ltd.
Milton Keynes UK
UKHW022141220422
401921UK00010B/599